© 2024 Dr. John D. McConnell. All rights reserved.

No part of this book may be reproduced, stored in a retrieval system, or transmitted by any means without the written permission of the author.

AuthorHouse™
1663 Liberty Drive
Bloomington, IN 47403
www.authorhouse.com
Phone: 833-262-8899

Because of the dynamic nature of the Internet, any web addresses or links contained in this book may have changed since publication and may no longer be valid. The views expressed in this work are solely those of the author and do not necessarily reflect the views of the publisher, and the publisher hereby disclaims any responsibility for them.

Any people depicted in stock imagery provided by Getty Images are models, and such images are being used for illustrative purposes only.
Certain stock imagery © Getty Images.

This book is printed on acid-free paper.

ISBN: 979-8-8230-3626-9 (sc)
ISBN: 979-8-8230-3627-6 (e)

Library of Congress Control Number: 2024922173

Print information available on the last page.

Published by AuthorHouse 11/13/2024

CONTENTS

Dedication v

Foreward ix

Introduction 3

Chapter 1   Check The Source 5

Chapter 2   Stop Avoiding The Mirror 16

Chapter 3   What's In Your Hand? 27

Chapter 4   Lead Without Conforming 38

Chapter 5   The Good Stuff Wins 50

Chapter 6   Parenting Older 59

Chapter 7   Yin and Yang 68

Chapter 8   As His Brother/Pastor 83

Chapter 9   An Unexecuted Vision 99

Chapter 10 The End Is Not Your Business 108

About the Author 123

DEDICATION

Most definitely my father had a quiet strength. He wasn't one to initiate telling a lot of stories. He was a good conversationalist, but I don't recall a time ever seeing him need the attention of an audience. Johnnie McConnell was an intent listener. No words got by him. Not only was he attentive to words, but he was very watchful. If my dad saw how something was done, it became something he could do. In turn, my father was a great teacher – however a very untraditional one.

Every day was a tutorial, because we never knew when our dad was going to ask us to do something he'd already shown us. He depended on us to pay attention because he wasn't big on wasting time. It was exciting to spend time with him, because you never knew what you might get to do that day.

I dedicate this book to my siblings (Carlton, Shirley, Mark, Janice, David, Dennis, and Christopher). Every time a story is told, it's from the perspective of the storyteller. My accounts of Dad may not totally mesh with your memories of specific events. Please know that if I got something wrong, it was not an attempt to embellish the truth. Penning this manuscript, I realized how difficult it is to tell your own story without monopolizing someone else's. I hope you don't feel misrepresented by any information I included.

I also dedicate this book to all those who are trying to make sense of having lost a parent too soon. The questions linger long after we've processed our grief. Where do I go from here? What is my value? It's natural to aspire to get a proverbial pat on the back from our parents. But where does the motivation come from to make them proud, if they're no longer here? I'd love to see my dad brimming with pride over how I turned out - every child wants that. The fact is, my value – your value was set in childhood. Although we thought we'd have the opportunity to gather more memories, the ones we have are truly all we need. Like a good house, we were built to last (with good bones).

IN HIS IMAGE

A Pattern to Live By

Johnnie McConnell
July 2, 1032 – February 8, 1990

FOREWARD

It has been an honor to sit and reflect on the life of my father. I am privileged to offer a glimpse of who I have become because of his essence. Although he transitioned this life at the age of forty-four, he instilled the core values I live by today. Part of the father's responsibility is to pass down life principles for generations to come. Although his time here was brief, I was fortunate to have acquired life skills, priceless wisdom, and the necessary keys to living a successful life.

Growing up, my father was a tough disciplinarian. There was a great deal I did not understand, but in his own way, he was preparing me for life. Now that I am older, I find myself mimicking him. Those attributes from my father are the driving force behind my success today. My work ethic, entrepreneur mindset and strength are because of him. He did not accept excuses, and I live the same way. Success is what I saw him achieve. Drive and determination are what he lived by. There are three major principles that I hold dear and incorporate into daily life. First, get up and make things happen. To me that means not depending on anyone - and if you want something, work hard to achieve or acquire it. You do not have to be jealous of the next person, just focus and put in the work to get it. Second, crying will not solve anything. You might receive a little sympathy, but it does not change the situation. Ask yourself, "What's the next move?" and keep pushing forward. You have the power to change the narrative. And lastly, all you have in life is your word. Stand on what you say. Be a man or woman of integrity.

I never saw defeat upon him. Even if he was down to his last dime, he did not show it. He taught me to look like a million dollars, whether you have it or not. See yourself in the place you want to be and pursue it. Even though he is not here physically, when I run across his former friends and family members, they often remind me of how much I resemble him. My drive definitely came from him.

IN HIS IMAGE

I have two daughters and a son of my own now and although they never met my dad personally, they have experienced his essence through me. I teach them the same principles I once learned. Actually, I do not stop with my children. Every young person I have the privilege of mentoring shares in the legacy of my father, and it will live on for generations to come.

My daughters are older than my son; however, shortly after he arrived, I realized I couldn't parent them all the same. Whether you're male or female, take notes as you digest the words John McConnell has included in this book. Father-daughter relationships have dynamics that differ from Father-son relationships, and Dr. McConnell sheds much light on that fact. Beyond having immense respect for this book's author, he and I have several points of connection. His dad and mine concluded their earthly journeys only 413 days apart, before our friendship began. I was twenty-four years old, and John was twenty-three. He and my late wife worked on several music recording projects together. John's sons and my daughters stairstep in age (twenty-five, twenty-four, twenty-three, and twenty-two). We've worked together in ministry thirteen years – the last six of which I've been his Pastor, and he our church's Minister of Music.

It has been thirty-three years, and a day does not go by without thoughts of him. I will forever cast a shadow of my father's silhouette and as long as his image is reflecting through me, he lives forever.

      Son of Willie C. McDuffie

      Efrem Z. McDuffie

INTRODUCTION

Having someone "good" to aspire to be like, is a great head start in life. Lots of boys I grew up around, were surrounded by males, but not all of them were good role models. The way my father lived, commanded my respect. He was genuinely a good person, not because he was my dad, but because he was good. None of us are without choices. To be good is a choice one must make consistently. It's a more difficult choice, because the road for those who choose to live a life without positive morals is wide and illuminated. We live in a culture that makes us feel justified when we're missing the mark.

As I interact with the people who regularly interact with my sons, they make a special effort to let me know how respectful they are. At nineteen, Jadden began inquiring about a Dodge Challenger he was interested in. He had been saving his money, but the process of purchasing a vehicle was foreign to him. Jadden was back-and-forth to the car lot asking all the pertinent questions. Most of what he needed, he didn't have, but over a period of about two months, he gathered the necessary paystubs and other documentation requested. It wasn't until then that I went to the car lot with him. Upon meeting the salesman, he told me that my son was remarkable to work with throughout the entire process. He said, "most kids your son's age come here dressed inappropriately, and don't know how to be respectful in a place of business. But through every phone call and face-to-face encounter, your son demonstrated that he's been raised with integrity". This is a regular occurrence when I shadow my sons during their endeavors. I'd be a fool to think I (or their mom) deserve all the credit. The rhythm of my life is intertwined with theirs. In part, my son's actions are the manifestations of how I've lived before them. I am who I am because of the nature of my father. My children lay claim to that same heritage. For me, WWJD stood for what would Johnnie do, long before it meant what would Jesus do.

CHAPTER I

CHECK THE SOURCE

A Pattern to Live By

- **Organic:** Relating to or derived from living matter -

History is attached to us all. Nothing of itself is "a new thing". Not knowing your past doesn't release you from it. A prerequisite for any doctor visit, is a health survey. What manifests in the lives of our parents is the best precursor for what's next for us. It's not always a direct correlation, but blood mimics blood.

Determining the value of anything begins with its origination. Auction houses will tell you that a great story is just as impactful as the facts when establishing interest amongst clients. I've even heard it said, "never let the truth get in the way of a good story".

What's your story?

Unless you're intrinsically motivated, the strength you need to accomplish your dreams, won't be activated. Accomplishing your "why" goes beyond grit, perseverance, and passion. The resolve of a person is determined by how few things are on their list for what they won't do to get what they want. Where does that type of drive come from? To thrive in the environments we live in today, you must have an edge. Simply being interested in accomplishment won't be enough. Knowing who you are, and that you belong in the spot you're fighting to be in, requires you to tap into a reservoir of hope and strength. Start asking the right questions so you can be empowered with your family story.

When I lost my dad thirty-four years ago, I had no idea what I still needed from him. The questions I asked my mom about him were superficial, as I was only twenty-two and hadn't embraced adulthood fully. I was thirty-eight when my mom died, with a five and three-year-old. As I am fast approaching the age my dad was when he left this life, there's so much intrigue I have. Some of my questions may never be answered. For instance, amongst fourteen siblings, was there any rivalry? Of my five siblings, there's one strained relationship. It grieves me that the connection has been lost for years, and I fear it will never be restored. In my youth, I never noticed a disconnect between my dad and his brothers and sisters. But I also never asked the question. When it was clear to me that I was losing the grip on my marriage, I wanted to counsel with my dad - WWJD? Although he had thirty-seven years of marriage with my mother, not once did we have a marriage conversation. Although I'm not acquainted with the details of my mom and dad's marriage, I'm familiar with the memories of them living it in front of me every day.

The relationship between fathers and sons is a complex tapestry woven with threads of tradition, identity, and shared experiences. Despite the diversity of human experience, certain commonalities persist across cultures and generations, shaping this fundamental bond. The passage of knowledge and values from father to son forms a cornerstone of this relationship. Whether through direct teachings, observations, or implicit modeling, fathers often play a crucial role in instilling cultural, moral, and practical wisdom in their sons. This transmission of knowledge not only ensures continuity across generations but also reinforces a sense of belonging and identity amongst certain groups of people.

Another significant commonality is the interplay of expectations and aspirations. Sons often look to their fathers as role models or benchmarks for their own development and achievements. This can manifest in various ways, from career choices influenced by paternal footsteps to personal goals shaped by familial values. Similarly, fathers may harbor hopes for their sons, projecting dreams unfulfilled or ambitions unrealized onto their offspring, thereby influencing their trajectories and choices. The dynamics of authority and guidance are pivotal in defining the father-son relationship. Traditionally, fathers have been seen as figures of authority and discipline, wielding influence over their sons' upbringing and decision-making processes. This authority, however, is not unidirectional; it often evolves into a more nuanced exchange of guidance and mutual learning as sons mature into adulthood. Fathers may find themselves learning from their sons' perspectives and experiences, thereby enriching their own understanding of parenthood and life itself.

Emotional resonance also underscores the bond between fathers and sons. Despite varying expressions of affection and communication styles, a deep emotional connection often exists, grounded in shared experiences of joy, sorrow, triumph, and loss. This emotional resonance can transcend words, finding expression in gestures, shared activities, or even moments of silence that speak volumes.

Furthermore, the passage of time and the inevitability of change contribute to the evolving nature of the father-son relationship. As sons grow into adulthood and potentially become fathers themselves, roles may reverse or redefine, prompting reflections on legacy, continuity, and generational shifts. This cyclical pattern emphasizes the interconnectedness of past, present, and future, highlighting the enduring impact of paternal influence across lifetimes.

Father-daughter relationships and father-son relationships, while both rooted in family expectations, often manifest in distinct ways due to our bonds to society, gender dynamics, and emotional dynamics unique to each pairing.

One notable difference lies in the traditional roles and expectations assigned to each gender within family structures. Historically, fathers have been perceived as providers and protectors, roles that may be interpreted differently when relating to daughters versus sons. Fathers often feel a heightened sense of responsibility to protect their daughters, reflecting societal attitudes towards female vulnerability and the need for paternal guardianship. This protective instinct can influence the dynamics of the relationship, fostering a nurturing and sheltering environment where daughters may seek comfort and security from their fathers.

Conversely, in father-son relationships, the emphasis may shift towards preparing sons for independence and resilience in a competitive world. Fathers may impart lessons on strength, stoicism, and perseverance, encouraging their sons to navigate challenges with resolve and self-assuredness. This factor can cultivate a sense of mentorship and camaraderie, where fathers and sons bond over shared pursuits and aspirations for achievement.

Moreover, communication styles often differ between father-daughter and father-son relationships, influenced by societal norms surrounding gender and emotional expression. Fathers may find themselves engaging in more emotionally intimate conversations with their daughters, providing a supportive space for discussing feelings, relationships, and personal growth. This open dialogue can foster a deep emotional connection, where daughters feel understood and validated by their fathers' attentiveness and empathy.

Father-son relationships may prioritize practical guidance and shared activities as avenues for bonding. Fathers and sons may unite over sports, hobbies, or professional endeavors, using these shared experiences to impart life skills and cultivate a sense of mutual respect and admiration. This shared camaraderie often reinforces a sense of identity and belonging within familial and societal frameworks, shaping the son's development and understanding of masculinity.

Furthermore, the dynamics of authority and independence may vary between father-daughter and father-son relationships. Fathers may navigate a delicate balance between fostering independence and offering guidance, particularly as daughters navigate adolescence and adulthood. This balance can influence daughters' perceptions of autonomy and self-reliance, as they navigate societal expectations and personal aspirations under their fathers' watchful guidance.

Anytime I was with my dad, I felt safe. It didn't matter where we were. Even if we weren't side-by-side, I knew exactly where he was in the room. As long as he was calm, I never felt worried or concerned. My dad was a calloused-hand man's man. When I was growing up, there were no YouTube tutorials for how to do things. The birthday of the Internet wasn't until 1983, when I was in high school. While fishing, I watched my dad put a hook through a worm, so I baited my hook the same way. After reeling in his catch, I watched him remove the hook from the fish's mouth, so I did the same. I was too busy impersonating my dad, to be fearful of things he wasn't threatened by. I remember one contract job we were working when I was sixteen. It was a beautiful office building in downtown Kansas City, Missouri. The maintenance crew discovered a rodent infestation, and identified a huge underground nest, adjacent to the building's foundation. With my dad's consultation, a fifty-five gallon drum of ammonia was delivered. We dug a hole two feet deep, and inserted a round aluminum vent duct as a funnel. After putting on green-filtered masks, we poured all fifty-five gallons of ammonia into the earth. The ground beneath us began to rumble as if we were standing on top of an active volcano. My dad had this look on his face I'd never seen before, and it made me feel like we shouldn't be there. My heart was racing and I was ready to sprint, but he didn't run, so I didn't either. After about two minutes, the rumble subsided and thank God, there was no eruption!

When confidence becomes an issue, it's good to have a body of work to consult. I succeed based on the challenges my family has championed. When we see things through the correct lens, a victory for one, is a victory for all. Being a successful author isn't an accolade I share alone. It should spark confidence in my children and grandchildren that it's within possibility for them as well. Traits and abilities aren't simply passed down just because there's a shared bloodline.

It can only manifest as an idea, unless you choose to embrace it as being yours. Doubt is completely legitimate unless or until you do something that defies it. Whether or not I could be an entrepreneur became a meritless doubt once I saw my dad do it. My inhibitions connected to being a good husband and father became meritless doubts once I saw my dad winning at it. Not having confidence to pursue my passions, became a meritless doubt after watching my father go for his.

CHAPTER II

STOP AVOIDING THE MIRROR

A mirror can only show you the image standing in front of it. While redefining what you see may be a helpful strategy, it doesn't change the image. Eventually, we must confront who's standing there. Seeing yourself for who you are is a difficult process, especially if you are unaware of your roots. Matter shares not only blood, but tendencies also. We are drawn to patterns of behavior, not merely because we lack self discipline, or self-control, but like a dolphin with echolocation, we sometimes find ourselves in situations we've been called to, but don't want to be part of. Behaviors that are random and occasional for some, are triggers for others. Things like schizophrenia, depression, and bipolar disorder get passed down from parents to children. Not confronting who you are and the symptoms you feel, can delay a very necessary diagnosis. As we learn of challenges, our family members have, we should pay attention to them as markers. I don't believe we should live in fear that every family plight will automatically transfer, but consider them a community from which to draw from.

Why Communities Are Important

Community plays a crucial role in the lives of family members, offering a multitude of benefits that contribute to their growth, well-being, and overall quality of life. From emotional support to social interactions and shared resources, the impact of community on families is profound and multifaceted.

One of the most significant benefits of community for family members is the emotional support it provides. Within a community, family members can find empathy, encouragement, and understanding during challenging times. Whether dealing with a personal crises, health issues, or everyday stressors, knowing that there is a network of people who care can alleviate feelings of isolation and loneliness. This support system enhances mental health by providing a safe space for expression and validation of emotions.

Communities often foster a sense of belonging, which is crucial for identity formation. When family members feel connected to a community, they are more likely to develop a positive self-image and a stronger sense of purpose. This sense of belonging can boost self-esteem and resilience, enabling family members to navigate life's ups and downs with greater confidence and optimism.

Communities offer ample opportunities for family members to establish and maintain social connections. Whether through neighborhood gatherings, religious institutions, or local clubs and organizations, families can interact with diverse groups of people who share common interests or values. These social dealings not only enrich personal lives but also provide networking opportunities that can lead to professional growth and career advancement.

For children and adolescents, community involvement promotes social skills development and peer relationships outside the immediate family circle. It exposes them to different cultures and perspectives, fostering tolerance and acceptance of diversity from a young age. These experiences lay a foundation for healthy social interactions and interpersonal communication skills that are essential for their future personal and professional relationships.

Communities function as resource hubs where family members can access practical support and resources. This may include childcare assistance, educational programs, healthcare services, and even financial aid during times of need. By pooling resources and expertise, communities empower families to overcome challenges that may otherwise seem insurmountable.

In close-knit communities, neighbors often look out for one another, creating a system of mutual aid and reciprocity. This informal support network can be invaluable during emergencies or unexpected life events, providing peace of mind and immediate assistance to family members facing crises situations. Shared resources such as libraries, community centers, and recreational facilities enhance the quality of life for families by offering affordable and accessible amenities near home.

Communities serve as repositories of cultural heritage and traditions, offering family members opportunities to celebrate and preserve their cultural identity. Festivals, rituals, and community events provide occasions for families to come together, strengthen bonds, and pass down cherished customs to future generations. These cultural experiences foster a sense of pride in one's heritage and promote intergenerational continuity within families. We also find that communities support educational enrichment through schools, libraries, and extracurricular activities that supplement formal learning. Family members benefit from access to educational resources and programs that promote lifelong learning and skill development. This educational support not only enhances individual academic achievement but also permits families to make informed decisions about their children's future and career aspirations.

There's data that links community involvement to improved physical health outcomes for family members of all ages. Engaging in regular physical activities such as community sports leagues or fitness classes promotes overall wellness and reduces the risk of chronic diseases. Additionally, communities often advocate for health promotion initiatives and provide access to healthcare services that address the specific needs of families, particularly in underserved or marginalized populations.

Thriving communities can influence health behaviors and lifestyle choices through peer support and collective efforts to create environments that prioritize health and safety. From promoting healthy eating habits to advocating for environmental sustainability, community-driven initiatives contribute to a healthier future for families and the broader community alike.

Participating in community activities instills a sense of civic responsibility and encourages family members to become active contributors to society. By volunteering, advocating for social causes, or participating in local governance, families demonstrate their commitment to making a positive impact on their community's well-being. This engagement fosters a sense of empowerment and civic pride among family members, reinforcing the importance of collective action and community solidarity. This collective involvement also promotes democratic values and civic engagement among children and youth, preparing them to become responsible citizens who are actively involved in shaping their communities and advocating for social justice. These experiences nurture leadership skills and a sense of social responsibility that are essential for building resilient communities and addressing shared challenges collaboratively.

If you look close enough into a mirror, it will show you things that are to come. This was never more apparent to me than in those moments when I was tasked to help my father with his razor bumps. It didn't happen often, as somehow it was Janice's role, but on the occasion when she wasn't home, and he'd catch me walking by his room, he'd yell out to me.

Very infrequently on a Saturday evening, while my parents watched television in their bedroom, my dad would ask me to 'pick his chin'. I can't recall ever seeing him with a beard, but he was never without a mustache. He used an electric shaver every morning for a nice clean cut. He had razor bumps beneath his chin and on his neck that wouldn't go away until the hair was removed from them with tweezers. He'd be lying on his back while I braced my left forearm across his chest, kneeling on the side of the bed with tweezers in my right hand. Up close and personal, I saw literally who I was growing to become. As I carefully extracted the hairs, I studied my dad's thick graying mustache, while noticing the hair thinning atop his head. We call it the family cul-de-sac. Many of the McConnell men fall victim of a balding pattern that allows a patch of hair growth at the top edge of the hairline. A bald semi circle forms behind it that resembles a circle drive. I started shaving my head at the age of forty, as that was around the time I became a member of the cul-de-sac club. As I noticed the fleshy bags underneath my dad's eyes, I remember thinking, "One day this will be me".

IN HIS IMAGE

A Glimpse

*Walking by the mirror, I gazed inside,
I noticed someone familiar, but he decided to hide, I stared inquisitively, hoping to discover the one there with me, He was definitely present – just very hard to see,
More light, I thought, that would make him appear, So I chose the larger mirror - underneath the chandelier,
Just as I thought – I'm not alone, That's my smile, but his jawbone, I made a slight adjustment to catch my profile, I was wearing his shoulders – no denial
After acknowledging the truth of what I was seeing, I was prompted to question my entire being, Now that I am intentional to notice his traces, I hear his cadence when I speak – I see him in my children's faces, Not only what I say convinces me he's here, But the way I speak is evidence dad is near,*

A Pattern to Live By

Here I was believing I'm living life alone, I'm thankful for the glance in the mirror that showed me I was wrong, No matter what life brings, I know I can survive, Because I now walk in the revelation that my hands are multiplied

By John McConnell

CHAPTER III

WHAT'S IN YOUR HAND?

A Pattern to Live By

A good first step towards deciding what vocation to aspire to, is paying attention to what you're good at. I watched my father plug into his gifts and talents to compete on an unlevel playing field. The 1960s was an especially difficult time for African-Americans, as the envelope was being pushed more and more for civil rights. Like many others, my dad had to fight the suppression of racism by being a stand-out. He understood the level of expectation put upon him, being black in the service industry. He was personable and disarming. Obtaining a contract to clean an office building occupied by only white employees in the early seventies, was easier said than done for a black man. People had to feel safe in their work environment, knowing the items at their workstation wouldn't be tampered with. People felt comfortable around my dad because he was a great conversationalist, and extremely reliable. To this very day, I am a stickler about being on time - because of my father's example. Being late, communicates your willingness to waste other people's time. Not only was my dad conscientious about time, but he made sure his work ethic was unmatched. He stayed abreast of sanitation trends, to always provide his clients a premium service. Surveillance cameras weren't prominent back then, but there was no shortage of hoops to jump through to prove your trustworthiness. Dad trained us to dress appropriately for office cleaning, and to assume that any valuables left on a desk was an intentional test of our integrity. After my dad secured his first cleaning contract, he never had to advertise to get more business (another of his alluring traits). Every additional contract was by referral. It's like when you see an extremely well manicured lawn. You want so bad to have your lawn look that way, and feel compelled to knock on the door and inquire about the landscaper. By the way, in addition to janitorial services, we also had a few landscaping contracts.

In the Bible (Zachariah 4:10), an angel of the Lord told the prophet, "**Do not despise these small beginnings, for the LORD rejoices to see the work begin**" In essence it's saying, whatever the task that looms before you, don't despise today ONLY because your initial efforts SEEM small and insignificant. Simple beginnings can grow to be so auspicious, and last for several generations. For example, in 1969, my father secured the cleaning contract at the Kansas Chamber of Commerce. Now, fifty-five years later, that contract is still in the family.

Focusing on your strengths is crucial for personal growth, fulfillment, and success in various aspects of life. It involves identifying and harnessing your innate talents, skills, and passions to achieve meaningful outcomes. Leveraging strengths enhances performance and productivity. When you concentrate on what you do best, tasks are completed more efficiently and with higher quality. This efficiency is not just about speed but also about producing outcomes that align with your highest potential. A gifted communicator (like my dad) excels in building relationships and influencing others, which are invaluable in leadership roles.

Focusing on strengths boosts confidence and motivation. Success breeds confidence, and when you excel in areas aligned with your strengths, you feel empowered to take on greater challenges. This positive reinforcement fuels intrinsic motivation, making it easier to persist through setbacks and uncertainties. Individuals who operate from a position of strength are often more resilient and adaptable in the face of adversity.

Emphasizing strengths encourages continuous learning and growth. Rather than fixating on weaknesses, which can be demoralizing and hinder progress, focusing on strengths fosters a growth mindset. It encourages seeking opportunities for development that build upon existing talents. This proactive approach to learning enhances skills organically, leading to mastery and innovation.

Additionally, concentrating on strengths promotes collaboration and teamwork. In diverse environments, individuals bring complementary strengths to the table, creating synergies that drive collective success. Recognizing and valuing each team member's strengths cultivates a culture of mutual respect and trust, essential for achieving common goals.

I remember my father, taking a keen interest in what fueled us as kids. He paid attention to what seemed to ignite us, and as best he could, facilitated our interests. I absolutely loved drums when I was a little boy. I remember destroying church fans and beating the air with the handles as though they were drumsticks. When I was in the fifth grade, somehow I convinced my dad to buy me a snare drum and a pair of sticks. At Quindaro Elementary we had a drill team that sometimes performed during school assemblies. They danced to records and cassettes, because our school had no band. I'll never forget the time they were invited to perform at the Southern Christian Leadership Conference parade.

A few of us guys who owned stationary snare drums convinced the girls that we could be their marching band. It didn't matter to us that we didn't have the proper equipment. We used belts and jump ropes to attach our drums to us. After a few years, my dad realized how serious I was about drums, and signed me up for lessons at Brady & Sons Music Store. Mr. Brady became my advocate, and convinced my dad that I needed a five piece drum set. One of the landscaping jobs we worked on Saturdays was at Kaw Valley Bank on Central Avenue. One Saturday after finishing that job, my dad surprised me by driving a few miles up Central Avenue to a place called Stinson's Music. We went inside, and I was allowed to pick out a drum set. It felt like Christmas! It's meaningful when your parents verbally support your interests, but when they financially invest in you beyond the basics of food, shelter, and clothes, the relationship goes to a whole new level. After the drummer at our church graduated high school and joined the military, I stepped into his role, playing drums for all four of our choirs. This caused me to get exposure along with all of my practice. I transitioned from being timid, to more confident. What I didn't realize then, was that I was becoming more confident overall. As a musician, singer, writer, student, and even around girls, I was coming into my own. Am I saying that if my dad had never purchased my drum set, I would've never become a confident person? Not at all. I'm simply acknowledging the legitimacy of parents tapping into the developmental assets of their children. There is also a significance in paying it forward and passing the baton. Although I never made a dime playing drums, both my sons expanded upon the foundation I gave them. They currently make a living playing drums and keyboards. I'm winning through them!

The more you live in someone's shadow, the longer it takes to cast your own. Although there were benefits growing up in a large family, there were also some negatives, like being sheltered. Strategy plays a huge role in the daily activities of a family of eight. The only reason we could travel in one vehicle was because federal laws didn't require child safety seats before 1985. Janice, myself, Dennis, and Christopher, are very close in age. All four of us were born within a five-year span. Can you imagine four car seats fitting in one vehicle? Not possible. It was on a rare occasion for us all to be in one car. We seldom went on road trips, but a few times we traveled to Louisiana for family reunions. Only our three-row station wagon could handle the numbers. Mom and dad occupied the front seat, with tiny Christopher sitting on the armrest. Shirley and Janice had the window seats on the second row, with Dennis in the middle. Mark and I sat on the back bench. Only one time did all eight of us board an airplane together. I was fifteen, and experienced the big city of Los Angeles for the first time. As a high school senior, I was selected to go on a seven-day trip to Washington DC to experience the political process up close in our nation's capital. The trip was sponsored by the school district for seven students, and it was the first time I was away from my family. It was then that I realized how sheltered my life had been. I was free to make my own choices outside of the opinions of my siblings. It felt amazing! That trip broadened my horizons, opening my eyes to careers I never knew existed. Some children grow up to work the same occupation as their parents because it's the only experience they've ever been made aware of.

Differing Interests

As we journey through life, we draw from so many different influences. What catches our attention doesn't always hold it, but if it does, there's a reason. My reason may differ dramatically from yours, despite how much we have in common. The polar differences between myself, Dennis, and Christopher amaze me. Our circumstances were identical, yet by fifth grade, it was obvious to me that our interests were not aligned. We were the last three kids born, each separated from the other by less than two years. We grew up virtually on top of one another, in a 1000 square-foot house. Imagine eight people cycling through one bathroom. All four boys shared one bedroom with two sets of bunkbeds. For time management and water conservation, my mom had Dennis, Christopher, and I take baths together every night. We received the same gifts for Christmas and on each other's birthdays for several years, to limit sibling rivalry. I vividly recall one Christmas, where there were three red tricycles with a harmonica on each seat. As close knit as we were, our aspirations for life grew further apart with each year. Even when adding Shirley, Mark, and Janice to the equation, no one took to singing like I did. We all enjoyed music, but I was the only one seemingly interested in playing instruments. Only I was attracted to theatre classes, and auditioning to be in plays and musicals. My parents proved that having a recipe for cooking is totally different than having a recipe for raising children. When preparing food, your dish will always come out the same as long as the recipe is strictly adhered to. It doesn't work that way at all with people. I had to experience parenting my own children in order to make some of the connections I couldn't see as an adolescent. At best, the most available father can only try to make the best adjustments to meet the needs of his children. There is always so much competing for their focus.

CHAPTER IV

LEAD WITHOUT CONFORMING

A Pattern to Live By

No matter what era you live in, there's always pressure to compromise. Unfortunately, being black in America has always meant living by a different set of rules. In most situations, we've been painted with stereotypes by people we've never met. We must work harder than others to ditch labels we never should've been assigned. I'm thankful that although the racism in my dad's era was more blatant, he didn't become bitter. Although the times were divisive, (and still are) conversations in our home were not laced with alienation. In my youth, my dad taught me how to interact with all people. He taught me that being respected requires me to show respect to others.

Johnnie McConnell valued results more than titles. He taught me that leaders lead even when they're not speaking. Leading from the back is a powerful approach that emphasizes empowerment, collaboration, and subtle guidance. It challenges the conventional notion that leadership is solely about holding a position of authority and instead highlights that true leadership involves influencing, inspiring, and supporting others. By understanding and embracing this concept, we can redefine what it means to be a leader and recognize that effective leadership often comes from the ability to guide and inspire from a position of support rather than dominance. This approach not only enriches the leadership experience but also contributes to more dynamic, innovative, and engaged teams and organizations.

A senior executive might have a title that signifies authority, but if they cannot inspire their team or garner their respect, their leadership effectiveness may be limited. Conversely, a team member without an official leadership title who consistently demonstrates expertise, integrity, and a collaborative spirit can exert significant influence and lead by example.

Having strong convictions isn't as celebrated as it once was. We've become desensitized to the horrible atrocities that occur in the world. An uptick in murder rates used to be an alarming statistic. We've grown accustomed to daily news that showcases deviant behaviors. Each family has a responsibility to stop normalizing behaviors that depict bad character and a lack of integrity. When we fail to address negative behaviors we witness in our adolescent children, we reinforce it. Where there are no boundaries, there is no discipline.

Every seasoned classroom teacher knows the importance of establishing rules on the first day of school. What's important to note, are the expectations. Effective discipline heavily relies upon a reward system. As a veteran teacher, I learned how powerful it was to discuss the positive consequences for meeting classroom expectations, before discussing the consequences for failing to meet them. When children understand the power of partnering in the discipline plan, the perspective becomes clearer for what they can earn, rather than what they can lose. Many parents approach discipline from the standpoint of taking things away. Depending on the personality of the child, that can easily backfire.

Holding to your convictions provides a source of resilience and motivation during difficult times. Leaders who adhere to their principles are better equipped to face opposition and setbacks with determination and resolve.

While adaptability is an essential trait for leaders, conformity—especially when it involves compromising personal convictions—can have detrimental effects. Conformity, driven by a desire to fit in or avoid conflict, can undermine effectiveness and the overall integrity of leadership.

Being anchored to one's convictions is a critical component of sustainable leadership. Convictions provide clarity and authenticity, essential for guiding people through challenges and changes. Conformity, on the other hand, can erase trust, compromise decision-making, and stifle innovation. Solid leadership also requires balancing conviction with flexibility. Leaders must navigate complex environments while upholding core values, cultivating supportive cultures, and embracing constructive feedback. By adhering to their principles while remaining adaptable, leaders can inspire trust, drive progress, and achieve lasting success.

Ultimately, the essence of leadership lies in the ability to lead with conviction, guided by a clear sense of purpose and unwavering commitment to core values. In doing so, leaders not only chart a path for their teams and organizations but also set an example of integrity and vision that can inspire and transform the world.

On occasion, my dad's good virtue left him holding the bag so to speak. Sometimes when you take a risk on others, you pay a price that leaves you with the short end of the stick. Many times as a landlord, my dad chose to be trusting when he probably should have been more practical. Following your heart when trying to help others is costly. My father chose to participate with the Section 8 housing program.

With government assistance, applicants who meet the requirements, are approved to rent houses from landlords who participate. The Section 8 office enters a contract detailing the specified amount it will pay and the amount the tenant will pay per month. Even with the government paying the lion's share of the rent each month, my dad sometimes struggled to receive payment from tenants when it was due. As you can imagine, there is a mindset that accompanies people who occupy property they have no stake in. While my dad's hope was to provide housing for people who couldn't otherwise afford a home, some tenets, abused the relationship, as well as the property. You wouldn't believe what we walked into after some evictions. From walls spray-painted with graffiti, to kitchen cabinets being pulled down to the floor, the disregard for our property felt inhumane.

It's easy to lose faith in humanity, and choose to not stick your neck out for those who don't seem to want better for themselves, but how can hopeless people climb out of the fray on their own? Age is not the only vindicator of a juvenile mindset. In most cases, people being sifted by life can't recognize the need for mentoring. Unless you're able to view help appropriately, you will abuse it.

In a world that often glorifies self-reliance and independence, seeking help can sometimes be perceived as a sign of weakness or inadequacy.

The first step in developing a healthy attitude towards receiving help is recognizing that it is a natural and often necessary part of life. Everyone, at some point, requires assistance from others. This need is not indicative of personal failure or incompetence but rather a normal part of human interdependence. Humans are inherently social beings who thrive in collaborative environments. From an evolutionary perspective, cooperation has been essential for survival and success. Recognizing this interdependence can help normalize the act of seeking and accepting support. Support networks, including family, friends, colleagues, and professionals, provide not just practical assistance but also emotional reinforcement. They contribute to personal growth, resilience, and overall well-being. Despite the inherent benefits of seeking help, several psychological barriers can make it difficult for individuals to acknowledge their need for assistance.

Many people worry about being judged or perceived as weak when asking for help. This fear can stem from societal expectations that value self-sufficiency and individualism. The perception that needing help is a personal flaw can deter individuals from reaching out. Individuals with low self-esteem may struggle with accepting help because they feel undeserving or believe that they should handle their problems on their own. This sense of inadequacy can hinder their willingness to seek support. Cultural norms can play a significant role in shaping attitudes towards help-seeking behavior. In cultures that emphasize stoicism and self-reliance, asking for help may be viewed as a failure or weakness. Some people avoid seeking help because they fear imposing on others or being a burden. They may believe that their problems are too trivial or that others are too busy to assist. Past experiences with help-seeking can influence current attitudes. If individuals have faced rejection or criticism when seeking help in the past, they may be hesitant to try again.

Strategies for developing healthy attitudes towards receiving support:

- Changing the perception of help from a sign of weakness to a natural and beneficial part of life can be empowering. Understanding that asking for help is a strength rather than a weakness can shift attitudes significantly. Support from others can lead to personal growth, learning opportunities, and enhanced problem-solving.

- Reflecting on personal attitudes and beliefs about having a deficit can uncover underlying fears and misconceptions. Self-awareness can help individuals recognize and address their discomfort with receiving assistance.

- Working on building self-esteem can make it easier to embrace help. This might involve setting and achieving small goals, practicing self-compassion, and challenging negative self-beliefs. When individuals value themselves and their needs, they are more likely to accept support graciously.

- Professional help can be invaluable in addressing deep-seated issues related to self-worth and help-seeking behavior. Therapists can provide strategies for overcoming resistance to receiving support and increase the development of healthier attitudes.

- Effective communication with potential supporters can alleviate fears about being a burden. By expressing needs clearly and acknowledging that support is welcomed rather than demanded, individuals can foster more positive and collaborative interactions.

- Understanding the positive impact of receiving help can motivate individuals to pursue it. Education on how support networks contribute to personal well-being and success can validate the importance of accepting generosity from others.

- Viewing help-seeking through the lens of empathy can shift perspectives. Recognizing that everyone needs relief, and that assisting others is a normal and positive aspect of relationships can encourage a more balanced view. Additionally, understanding that offering support in return can create mutually beneficial relationships.

- Engaging in conversations about societal expectations and norms regarding self-reliance and expressing a need for a hand up can help shift cultural attitudes. Promoting a more accepting and supportive culture can reduce the stigma associated with receiving help.

CHAPTER V

THE GOOD STUFF WINS

A Pattern to Live By

Always purpose to allow your absolute best to speak for you. At its core, allowing the best of you to speak for you means embracing authenticity. Authenticity is not merely about being truthful; it is about being congruent with your inner values and beliefs. When we align our actions with our true selves, we naturally attract those who appreciate us for who we are. This principle operates under the belief that authenticity breeds trust. When others sense that you are genuine, they are more likely to engage with you, collaborate, and share in your vision.

To cultivate this authenticity, self-awareness is essential. Understanding your strengths, weaknesses, passions, and values lays the groundwork for presenting your best self. Engaging in practices like journaling, meditation, or seeking feedback from trusted friends can deepen your self-knowledge. For instance, consider what moments in your life made you feel most alive or fulfilled. These reflections can provide insight into the qualities that define your best self.

Once you have a clearer understanding of who you are, the next step is to express that identity in a manner that resonates with others. Communication plays a pivotal role in this process. The way you articulate your thoughts and feelings can either amplify your authenticity or obscure it. For example, in a professional setting, you may feel pressured to conform to a certain image or style. However, the most effective communicators are those who blend professionalism with personal flair, ensuring their unique voice shines through.

This principle applies equally in personal relationships. When you allow the best of you to speak in conversations, you foster deeper connections. Sharing your passions, dreams, and even vulnerabilities invites others into your world, creating a bond built on transparency.

What About Hope?

What is both profound and transformative is that my being hopeful is tied to my positive outlook on life. Hope serves as a guiding light, illuminating pathways to potential futures and empowering individuals to pursue their aspirations despite challenges. By fostering hope through goal-setting, social support, and positive thinking, individuals can cultivate resilience and maintain a positive perspective on life. Embracing hope not only enhances personal well-being but also contributes to a more optimistic and fulfilling existence.

In the movie, "Cold Copy", one character asks another, " How are you able to remain so positive?" The response - "I believe the good stuff wins!" How we see things is how the story goes. Since it's ours to tell, I choose to spin everything in my favor.

The thing that defines every battle is how it ends. Every competitor entering a race, has victory on their mind. Achieving goals is what justifies the struggle. A key component to how we're wired is tied to what motivates us.

The pleasure center of the brain plays a crucial role in how we experience and seek pleasure. This system is part of the brain's reward circuit, which is essential for reinforcing behaviors that are critical for survival and well-being.

When we engage in activities that we find rewarding, such as eating, socializing, or winning a competition, the brain releases neurotransmitters like dopamine. Dopamine is often associated with pleasure and reward.

The reward system operates on a principle of positive reinforcement. When an action leads to a pleasurable outcome, the brain encodes this experience as positive, making us more likely to repeat the behavior in the future. This is particularly evident in competitive scenarios where the desire to win drives individuals to exert significant effort and persistence.

In a competition, the prospect of winning activates the brain's reward system. The anticipation of success and the pleasure associated with achieving a goal can be powerful motivators. When a competitor envisions victory, dopamine is released, which enhances focus, energy, and motivation. This chemical boost not only makes the prospect of winning more appealing but also reinforces the desire to engage in behaviors that increase the likelihood of success.

The process of preparing for and competing in a contest involves considerable effort and strategic planning. Competitors often train rigorously, practice specific skills, and adopt strategies aimed at outperforming others. This hard work is fueled by the brain's reward system, which creates a feedback loop: the more effort and dedication invested, the greater the anticipation of reward, which in turn drives even more effort. This reward system also helps in managing the stress and challenges associated with competition. The drive to achieve a goal can act as a buffer against feelings of frustration or setbacks. By focusing on the potential rewards and the pleasure of winning (the good stuff), individuals are often able to persist through difficulties and remain committed to their goals.

This intricate relationship between pleasure, effort, and reward explains why individuals might push themselves to extraordinary lengths in competitive environments. When engaged this way, the brain not only motivates but also reinforces behaviors that align with achieving desirable outcomes. Winning a competition is not merely about the tangible prize but also about the intense pleasure and satisfaction derived from the accomplishment, which further fuels the drive for success.

Conversely, some situations that have a proven record of toxicity, are able to compel a continued partnership.

Allegiance to toxic relationships is often a complex interplay of psychological investment, emotional attachment, fear of the unknown, social and cultural pressures, hope for change, self-esteem issues, cognitive dissonance, and dependency. Understanding these factors can provide insights into why people may struggle to leave unhealthy relationships and underscore the importance of supportive interventions and resources to help them make healthier choices.

Identifying the correlations between my dad's life and my own, doesn't mean I agree with every decision he made. What son has never bumped heads with his father? There were many things we saw differently. I was a very opinionated adolescent, and far from getting my way more than half the time. For instance, I was a phenomenal student in school, and applied to several colleges abroad. It was my desire to go away to college, but I only received partial academic scholarship offers from a few schools. In the end, my heart was set on attending Wichita State University – mainly because my girlfriend at the time was attending that school. UMKC was offering a larger scholarship, and my dad said it only made sense for me to go there, commuting each day from home. Since he was making the financial commitment, I really didn't have a choice; however, I hated his decision. I exercised a silent rebellion, and attended UMKC with Lil to no enthusiasm. Although I completed my undergraduate degree at Saint Mary College, UMKC was the right fit for me at the time. I made several weekend road trips to WSU chasing the excitement I thought I was missing. Let's just say our imagination sometimes paints a better picture than reality. The disagreements are not what I carry with me today. Even when we were at odds, there was never a time I didn't believe my father had my best interest at heart. Dwelling on cloudy days, never ushers in the sunshine. I choose to shake off negativity, and only allow the good stuff to reside in my heart.

Speaking of cloudy days and sunshine, I believe God helps us flip the switch, when we can't do it on our own. After my father passed unexpectedly February 8, 1990, that date each year represented deep sorrow. Ten years later, February 8, 2000, my son Jarrett was born. His birth didn't erase the memory of my dad's death, but it gave my family something beautiful to replace the sorrow with. I'll never forget how much joy my son being born on that day, brought not only my immediate family, but my mother as well.

CHAPTER VI

PARENTING OLDER

A Pattern to Live By

59

Like my father, I was in my thirties when my children were born. I don't have a youthful memory of my dad. He always seemed old to me. When I tried out for my first organized sports team in the fifth grade, my dad was already forty-six, and age fifty when I won a spot on my freshman high school basketball team. With my dad's jobs and the roles he filled at church, there wasn't much gas left in the tank. Time spent with him was always meaningful, but.

heavy on practical lessons. Before I was a teenager, I knew that fuel oil was good for removing scuffs from floors, and baling wire was good for tying together freshly pruned tree limbs. I knew how to use a commercial buffer to strip and polish floors, and shampooing carpet was something I could do in my sleep. I loved learning from my dad, but the fun things I learned from my older brother, or I had to teach myself. As I began learning new skills on my own, I found it exciting to share those skills with others. I taught both of my younger brothers how to swim, and how to shoot layups with their left hand. As a teen, I realized I was good at teaching songs, and begin to do that more and more at church. These were all baby steps towards me later embracing becoming a schoolteacher.

Starting a family is a monumental decision that profoundly impacts couples' lives. Traditionally, the timing of starting a family was aligned with societal norms and economic stability. However, in recent decades, there has been a notable shift towards couples waiting until later in life to have children. Today's average age of first-time parents is twenty-seven. This delay in starting a family has become increasingly common and is influenced by various factors such as career aspirations, financial stability, and personal development. Let's explore the benefits of couples waiting until later to start their family, examining how this trend impacts individuals, relationships, and society as a whole.

One of the primary benefits of delaying parenthood is the opportunity for personal and professional growth. In the past, early parenthood often meant sacrificing educational and career pursuits. Today, couples, particularly women, have greater access to education and career opportunities than ever before. Waiting to have children allows individuals to establish themselves in their careers, pursue higher education if desired, and achieve financial stability. This not only benefits the parents but also enhances the overall well-being of the family unit. Research indicates that children born to parents who are financially stable tend to have better access to resources and opportunities, which can positively impact their development and future prospects. Waiting to start a family can have significant benefits for the emotional and psychological well-being of parents. Parenthood is both rewarding and challenging, requiring considerable emotional maturity and resilience. Couples who delay parenthood often have more time to strengthen their relationship, establish effective communication patterns, and address any potential conflicts or concerns. This emotional preparedness can contribute to more stable and supportive parenting dynamics, which are crucial for the healthy development of children.

Additionally, delaying parenthood can lead to more informed and intentional family planning decisions. Couples who wait until later in life to have children are more likely to have thoughtfully considered factors such as family size, parenting styles, and childcare arrangements. This foresight can contribute to a more cohesive family unit and reduce stress associated with unexpected challenges or transitions.

From a societal perspective, the trend towards delayed parenthood can have several positive implications. For instance, individuals who delay having children tend to contribute more actively to the workforce and economy during their early adulthood. This can lead to increased productivity and innovation, benefiting the overall economy. Delaying parenthood can also help alleviate some of the financial pressures on social welfare systems by reducing the number of young families in need of support.

Waiting longer can have positive implications for public health. Research suggests that older parents may be more likely to have access to healthcare services and resources that contribute to healthier pregnancies and better maternal and child health outcomes. Abstinence or intentional waiting, reduces the incidence of teenage pregnancy and unplanned pregnancies, which are associated with higher rates of maternal and infant health complications.

However, it is important to acknowledge that there are also challenges associated with delaying parenthood. For instance, fertility declines with age, particularly for women, which can increase the likelihood of infertility or difficulty conceiving. Advances in reproductive technology have provided options for couples facing infertility challenges, but these options can be costly and emotionally taxing.

Not long ago, I went to YouTube to get instructions for washing chicken before cooking it. I had to toggle between several videos, because I learned that there's an old-school versus new-school debate over the whole idea. Some say that when you remove chicken from its grocery store packaging, you should go through several steps to adequately wash off bacteria. Another camp says to skip the washing - the proper heat temperature when cooking, will kill any lingering microorganisms. They say we introduce bacteria like salmonella to our sinks, counters, and every cleaning utensil we use in which to "prep" the chicken.

The chicken-washing debate made me think about older parents a little differently. If washing raw chicken can be linked to the spread of germs, is it also possible that parenting children too young can put the child in more eminent danger, due to a lack of safeguards? This may be a stretch, but for a moment let's compare the process of building people to the process of building homes. Usually, when referring to something as having good bones, the conversation is about a solid, sturdy foundation. When building anything, it's important to factor in what may come against it later. Building permits and inspections are fundamental aspects of any construction process, ensuring that both residential and commercial structures meet safety standards, regulatory requirements, and community expectations. The primary purpose is to advocate the safety of occupants and the public. Building codes, which permits and inspections enforce, establish minimum standards. These codes cover a wide range of concerns, including structural integrity, fire precautions, and electrical and plumbing systems.

The risk of accidents, injuries, and fatalities would significantly increase without the protocols, making the rules of construction crucial for public safety.

Adhering to the "construction code of conduct" contributes to the creation of high-quality, durable structures that stand the test of time. Factoring in the possibility of the most devastating natural events (tornadoes, hurricanes, earthquakes, and floods) is what ensures that structures are built effectively.

No individual is responsible for the choices people make once they've grown into adulthood. No one gets the blame for what went wrong, nor the credit for the good stuff. The only job you have as a youngster is to absorb as much as you can from what surrounds you. In our adolescence, we're challenged to discern good from bad. Of course it's beneficial to have great role models to assist with guidance, but ultimately our walk is by choice. I had the good fortune of having a father whose light illuminated bright. Other influences may have added, or competed, but nothing drowned out his voice in my life. When you're alone with your thoughts, whose voice do you hear? If you disagree with the character of those who speak into your life, find a more compelling voice to submit to. Just as important as it is to have property owners, developers, and local authorities contributing to the creation of resilient, high-quality buildings and vibrant, well-planned communities, every human life fairs better from the input of a strong village. Receive that for your life, then pay it forward in your service to others.

CHAPTER VII

YIN AND YANG

A Pattern to Live By

My dad met a cute sixteen year old named Jimmie Mae Grimes. He told her he was going to Kansas City to find a good job, and that he'd return to marry her. In August of 1952, my mom and dad were married in front of her Uncle Jack's gas station in Lillie, Louisiana. She was seventeen and he was twenty. Neither of them garnered a formal education, but hard work was not foreign to them. They made a great team. He was a bit introverted with a hard shell, and she softened him with her high energy. Although very eager to get their family underway, life threw them some wicked curveballs. As a young couple, they endured their share of grief - experiencing six failed pregnancies. Grandma Macie passed away and home-life shifted dramatically in Louisiana. Some of my dad's siblings were still quite young at that time, and the older ones stepped up to share the load. My mom and dad welcomed Aunt Clemontine and Uncle James into their home, and enrolled them in elementary school. My parents supported Aunt Tina until she moved to California to live with Uncle Cleo's family. Not long after I came along, my

Uncle James moved out to attend college at Emporia State University. I was a teenager before I was able to distinguish whether "J" was my brother or uncle.

It was filling improbable that my parents were going to be able to have children of their own, so in 1960, they adopted my oldest brother, Carlton (at birth). As life would have it, only a few months after Carlton came home, my mom got pregnant with Shirley, and successfully gave birth in December of 1961. The floodgate was open and all six miracle babies were born within 10 years (1961 - 1971).

I'd like to think the experience of having grieved together from so much loss, made my parents' bond stronger. That makes for a great story. But what I can say with certainty, is that they definitely used it to help them choose one another every day. Consistently choosing one another like they did, made them strive to be the parents I needed growing up.

Choosing Each Other Daily

Marriage is often portrayed as a union sealed by vows, but its strength and longevity hinge on a daily choice: the decision to continue loving, supporting, and cherishing one another. This act of choosing each other daily forms the bedrock of a resilient and fulfilling marital bond, transcending mere commitment into a continual practice of love and partnership.

Married couples who actively choose each other daily prioritize their relationship amidst life's inevitable challenges and distractions. This intentionality involves small gestures of affection, genuine communication, and shared experiences that reinforce their connection. Each day presents new opportunities to reaffirm love, whether through a heartfelt conversation over breakfast, a supportive text during a busy workday, or a shared laughter-filled moment before bed. These intentional acts not only strengthen the emotional bond but also foster a sense of security and mutual appreciation.

Choosing each other daily nurtures emotional intimacy, which is vital for marital satisfaction and resilience. Couples who consistently invest in understanding each other's feelings, dreams, and fears create a safe space for vulnerability and empathy. This emotional connection acts as a buffer during times of stress or conflict, fostering understanding and a deeper bond. Through shared experiences and open communication, couples build a reservoir of trust and companionship that sustains them through life's inevitable ups and downs.

Respect forms a cornerstone of healthy marriages, and daily choices to honor and value one another reinforce this foundation. By actively listening, appreciating each other's perspectives, and supporting individual growth, couples cultivate a climate of mutual respect. This respectful attitude extends to decision-making processes, conflict resolution, and even mundane daily interactions, fostering a partnership where both spouses feel valued and understood.

Physical intimacy is another aspect of marriage that benefits from daily choice. Beyond its obvious role in expressing love and desire, physical closeness strengthens emotional bonds and promotes overall well-being. Couples who prioritize physical affection and intimacy communicate their desire and commitment non-verbally, reinforcing the emotional connection and fostering a deep sense of belonging.

Marriage inevitably faces challenges, from external pressures to internal conflicts. Choosing each other daily equips couples with resilience to navigate these challenges as a unified team. Whether facing financial hardships, career changes, or family crises, spouses who prioritize their relationship find strength in each other's support and encouragement. This shared resilience not only deepens their bond but also enhances their ability to overcome adversity together, emerging stronger and more united.

Daily acts of choosing each other cultivate gratitude within marriage. Recognizing and expressing appreciation for each other's contributions, whether big or small, fosters a positive marital climate. Gratitude reinforces the value each spouse brings to the relationship and encourages a cycle of kindness and generosity. By focusing on the positives and expressing gratitude, couples create a nurturing environment where love and appreciation thrive.

Married couples who prioritize daily choices in their relationship serve as role models for others, including their children, family, and friends. By demonstrating mutual respect, commitment, and love through their actions, they inspire those around them to cultivate healthy relationships in their own lives. This ripple effect extends beyond the couple themselves, contributing positively to their broader community and fostering a culture of strong, supportive relationships.

IN HIS IMAGE

A Pattern to Live By

The Impact of Loss

While marriage thrives on daily choices to love and support, the experience of profound loss, such as the death of a child, can profoundly impact a relationship. In the face of devastating grief, couples often find themselves navigating uncharted emotional territory together. The loss of a child shakes the very foundation of a marriage, testing its resilience and highlighting the depth of their bond.

Experiencing loss together can deepen empathy between spouses as they navigate the complex emotions of grief. Each partner's unique response to loss may vary, yet the shared experience fosters a profound understanding of each other's pain and coping mechanisms. This empathy forms a bridge of support, allowing spouses to lean on each other during moments of overwhelming sorrow and vulnerability.

The loss of a child can prompt couples to reevaluate their priorities and rediscover their shared purpose in life. Confronting mortality often leads to introspection about what truly matters, strengthening the resolve to cherish their relationship and support each other through healing. This shared journey of finding meaning amidst loss reinforces their commitment to each other and reaffirms their shared values and goals.

Effective communication becomes crucial as couples navigate grief together. Honest dialogue about their feelings, fears, and hopes allows spouses to provide mutual comfort and validation. Vulnerability in sharing their pain and memories fosters a deeper emotional connection, paving the way for healing and eventual acceptance. Through open communication, couples reaffirm their commitment to each other's well-being and forge a path toward recovery together.

While grief tests the resilience of a marriage, facing loss together can ultimately strengthen the bond between spouses. The shared experience of overcoming profound sorrow fosters resilience and fortitude, equipping couples with the tools to weather future challenges as a unified team. This newfound strength reinforces their commitment to each other and empowers them to face life's uncertainties with courage and solidarity.

To use a football analogy, my dad was the coach of our team, but my mom, most certainly was the quarterback. Dad communicated the outcome he wanted to see, while mom stroked the ego and provided the proper motivation for the tasks to be completed. I always appreciated that if there was ever anything too difficult to discuss with my dad, mom was always available.

I've always wanted to emulate what I saw as the best parts of my mom and dad. Watching her lead songs in our church choir, was probably what gave me the desire to step forward and sing in church. If we're honest, most kid's public participation begins with attention-seeking. My mom loved to sing, and I knew that if I volunteered to lead a song in the youth choir, she'd be impressed with me.

The male chorus was responsible for music at my church only one Sunday each month. Although my dad wasn't a great singer, the choir wasn't something he backed down from. Finding bonding time with my dad was a strategic process. He stayed on the go, so the best option was to find a way to jump into his flow. Imagine six siblings ages seven to fifteen competing for daddy time. I was ten years old, and the only one of us who truly enjoyed singing.

I thought it would be awesome to join my dad's choir, and be the only one allowed to ride in the car with him to rehearsals.

Mount Zion Male Chorus

When I was twelve, my dad drove me to school on his way to work. I was in the seventh grade. He had a 1974 Ford Pinto stick shift. He never instructed me to watch him drive, but it was expected. We had a station wagon that my mom drove, but the Pinto was my dad's "work car". It was what they call a 'hot mess'. There was room for only one passenger. There were back seats, but you never saw them because of all of the cleaning equipment and supplies my dad kept stored inside. When closing the hatchback door, we were always careful not to slam it, for fear of a buffer wheel or mop handle cracking the glass. I don't recall a time my mom ever rode in my dad's Pinto.

A Pattern to Live By

Dr. John D. McConnell

A Pattern to Live By

CHAPTER VIII

AS HIS BROTHER/PASTOR

A Pattern to Live By

Clemontain Horn (Aunt Clemmie)

There were nearly thirteen years between Johnnie and I. When Johnnie was twenty-two I went to live with him and Jimmie Mae in Rosedale, Kansas, as a fourth-grader. I was nine years old. Johnnie always worked a little too hard. He left out early and came in late. My younger brother, James Daniel, was alsold there with me those two years. They didn't have any children yet, as they had only been married a short while. I remember how beautifully my sister-in-law carried herself. I loved the way she dressed. One time in fifth grade, I did something so mischievous, that the school had to call Jimmie to come up. I wanted everyone at school to see how pretty she was. I wanted them to see the style in which she dressed. She couldn't have been more than 19 years old at the time, but she was my brother's treasure. In those days, cigarette smoking had become quite popular, and my sister-in-law was determined to move with the trends. Johnnie, equally determined that Jimmie was not going to be a smoker, found those hidden packs of cigarettes every place she hid them - and ripped them to pieces in front of her. I'm sure that not only prevented her from becoming addicted to cigarettes, but caused me to never see smoking as an option for my life. I can truly thank my brother for that. Although Johnnie was constantly working, he made it a point that we all consistently attended church. Every Sunday service, and Wednesday Bible study, we were there. The meals at my brothers house were extraordinary. We ate well every day, but on Sundays it was super special. We always sat together at the dinner table - talking, laughing, and eating. There was always plenty, as my brother was a good provider.

A Pattern to Live By

James Daniel McConnell (Uncle J)

What A Man!

*"Get wisdom! Get understanding!
Do not forget or turn away from the words of my mouth.
Do not forsake her, and she will preserve you.
Love her, and she will keep you.
Wisdom is the principal thing; Therefore, get wisdom.
And in all your getting, get understanding."
Proverbs 4: 5-7*

Johnnie McConnell was one of the wisest men that I have had the privilege of knowing. His business acumen was sharp and keen because of his wisdom. My brother, Johnnie, had more influence on me than all my other siblings. He moved to Kansas City, Kansas from Vernon, LA in 1951 and participated in the "lucrative" business of the Kansas City Flood Cleanup project of 1951. He was employed a short time at the Fulton Bag Company and for twelve years at the Nutrena Feed Mill. Afterwards, he became employed in the

Kansas City, Kansas Public School System. My brother was a hardworking man. He taught me the value of hard work, and not to depend on others for a handout.

I moved to Kansas City from Vernon, Louisiana in 1952, after the death of my mother, Macie McConnell. I lived with my second oldest brother, Houston, and his wife, Niona. I started kindergarten that fall at Douglass Elementary. The next year, I moved with my brother, Johnnie and his lovely wife, Jimmie Mae. We lived at "Mr. Cunningham's Place" in Rosedale, 2634 S.15th Lane. From there, I attended Attucks Elementary and Noble Prentis Elementary.

My older brothers, who had already relocated to Kansas City, encouraged my father, Mack McConnell, Sr., to relocate to Kansas City as well. He did, but it took him a while to locate a place to live for all the younger siblings, and employment to adequately provide for all the younger siblings. It was decided that we would be split up into the homes of the older boys. My sister, Tina and I were to live with Johnnie and Jimmie.

When Dad found adequate housing and became gainfully employed, I moved in with him.

Johnnie and Jimmie were God-fearing people and gave their hearts and lives totally in service to God. They were members of Mt. Zion Baptist Church in Kansas City, Kansas. Because of his Christian character, honesty, wisdom, and his devout faith in God, Reverend M.E. Ford, Pastor, set Johnnie aside to become a deacon and serve on the Deacon Board in 1956. He possessed all the attributes of a deacon, as outlined in 1Timothy 3: 8-12. "They must be grave, not double-tongued, not given to much wine, not greedy of filthy lucre, and be husbands of one wife, ruling their children and their own houses well." After the passing of Deacon Marshall Tabor, Chairman of the Deacon Board, my brother Johnnie became the new Chairman. He served faithfully until his death in 1990. I am so blessed that I made the decision to accept Jesus Christ as my Lord and Savior, join Mt. Zion, and be baptized, also in 1956. My big brother always referred to me and introduced me as his "kid brother." I always found that to be his term of endearment to me.

Johnnie and Jimmie for many years did not have children that they had birthed. They adopted Carlton Dwight, and afterwards, the floodgates opened. Six children were born beginning with Shirley Ann on December 29, 1961. Johnnie and Jimmie loved each one of them equally. Carlton brought joy and happiness to everyone that he encountered. Carlton's mission on earth came to an end on April 22, 1971, as he passed away on this date.

My daddy passed away on November 13, 1962. I was in 8th grade at that time, and once again, my brother Johnnie and his wife, Jimmie, welcomed me back into their home. Not long after, he "cast his line" and started his own McConnell Cleaning and Janitorial Service, a very successful entrepreneurship.

I enjoyed immensely being a member of the Johnnie McConnell household. I enjoyed the kids looking up to me as their big brother. When some of them discovered that I was their uncle, not their brother, this brought about tears, disappointment, and unhappiness. I learned to drive by driving the family car, a 1956 Chevrolet Belair. My brother allowed me to drive that Chevrolet to my Senior Class Homecoming. I lived with Johnnie and Jimmie until I went away to attend my junior and senior year in college. I became engaged and married Mary Ellen Harris on June 1, 1969. Since I had not reached the age of 21, I had to get a signature from an adult to grant me permission to get married. My brother, Johnnie affixed his signature approving the marriage.

In November 1971, Mt. Zion welcomed Rev. C.L. Bachus as its new pastor. As Chairman of the Deacon Board, Johnnie prayerfully led the search committee that sought and found our new pastor. Our church was abundantly blessed under his pastorate. Pastor Bachus retired in 2023 after fifty-one plus years as pastor. Johnnie's name is affixed on the cornerstone of two wings of the church. He made a huge difference in the lives of so many family members, church members, and certainly members of the Kansas City, Kansas Public School System.

Johnnie died suddenly on February 8, 1990. I was conducting a leadership class at a downtown hotel when I received a devastating phone call stating that my brother had died. That was some news that shook me to my very core. His funeral service was attended by so so many people. He certainly meant a great deal to many individuals.

WHAT A MAN Johnnie McConnell was!

C. L. Bachus (Pastor)

For nearly fifty-two years I served as the pastor of Mount Zion Baptist Church in Kansas City, Kansas. It's not hyperbole that my family may never have planted roots in Kansas City had it not been for Johnnie McConnell. After Reverend M. E. Ford embraced his new position as Pastor at a church in Colorado Springs, Colorado, Mount Zion was left without a pastor.

When 1971 began, I was the Pastor of New Light Baptist Church in Helena, Arkansas. James Hawkins, who was a member of Mount Zion in Kansas City, came home to visit the Bobo family in Helena where I was pastoring. That was when he met me at New Life Baptist Church. Later that year, after Pastor Ford took his exit from Mount Zion, James Hawkins got busy talking to Deacon Johnnie McConnell and other church members about the young man he had met earlier that year in Helena, Arkansas. Brother Hawkins and Johnnie McConnell (chairman of the Deacon ministry) initiated contact to ascertain my interest in relocating to Kansas City, Kansas. Deacon McConnell called me and invited me to come to Kansas City and preach as a candidate to become pastor of the church.

On the weekend of the third Sunday in October of 1971, my brother, Deacon Charles Henry Bachus, and I made a visit to the heart of America. I met with the church officers on the Saturday preceding that Sunday service. And on Sunday morning I preached what God gave me. Late Friday night, nearly three weeks later, Deacon McConnell called to inform me that Mount Zion had met and arrived at the decision to empower me as their next pastor. Just one short month after my inaugural visit to Kansas City, I (and my wife, Wilma) returned to officially accept the position as pastor of the church.

On a late Saturday afternoon, Wilma and I met with the deacons and trustees at the home of Deacon McConnell. We had dinner with the officers and their wives.

On that third Sunday morning in November, Deacon Johnnie McConnell announced that I had accepted the call to become the new pastor of Mount Zion Baptist Church.

I preached that Sunday, and Wilma and I left and drove back home to Arkansas. I only communicated with Deacon McConnell until I moved my family Thursday, December 17, 1971. The evening we arrived in Kansas City, we were surprisingly greeted by many of the church officers and their wives. (Deacons: Johnnie McConnell, Ira Nicholson, John McCloyn, Lee Fraser, Charles Douglas, and Mack Whiting

Trustees: Eddie Fears, Jr, Eugene Marshall, Willie Smith, and Sam Bagsby)

It was a gracious welcome, awaiting us at the church parsonage located at 1720 Cleveland Avenue, Kansas City, KS 66104.

Beyond a shadow of doubt, Johnnie McConnell was one of the finest Christian men I have ever known. I served as his pastor from that time, until he left this earth February 8, 1990. I was honored when asked by his son, John David, to share some of my memories of pastoring his dad and my friend.

For all that he meant to me and the Mount Zion church family, I could easily recount enough details of our eighteen year relationship to fill a book of my own. From the moment we hit town, Johnnie and Jimmie were tremendous friends to Wilma and I - and our kids were roughly the same ages.

Every Pastor's life would be better served if he had a servant-leader and friend like Johnnie. He was a great example for other men who served along with him. He led by example, and never asked anyone to make sacrifices he wasn't willing to make.

As Pastor, I led the church to undertake many programs and projects that improved and expanded our church ministry and community. Brother McConnell would sometimes say, "Reverend I don't quite understand how that's going to come out, but you have a history of success, so I trust that you have it all worked out. Therefore, I will do all I can to support your proposal". The last major project that I discussed with Deacon McConnell, he said to me, "Pastor I am not trying to run your business, but whatever else you have planned for this church to accomplish, you'd better try and get it done before you get too old. You are not going to feel like having all the pressure on you as you get older". I am referring to the east fellowship hall, and Sunday church school building.

Deacon McConnell didn't witness the completion of this project, but would have been really happy with how we were able to meet our goal. It's my belief that Saints that pass on before us know what's going on here on earth, so I'm sure he is happy about the success of our church.

It's my opinion that any local church would be greatly blessed to have a Consequential Leader like Deacon Johnnie McConnell. God made him a little lower than the angels. He was definitely one of God's chosen saints. It isn't possible for my lifespan to outgrow my gratefulness to God for planting Johnnie McConnell in my pastoral ministry. Somehow or another brother McConnell knew his time was short, as he asked me if Deacon James Douglas could serve in his place as Chairman, should the need arise. Like clockwork, Deacon

Douglas picked up the mantle and has demonstrated the very same qualities Deacon McConnell exemplified while he lived.

Pastor, Dr. Clemmie Lee Bachus
Mount Zion Baptist Church

CHAPTER IX

AN UNEXECUTED VISION

A Pattern to Live By

In a perfect world, this chapter would include a testimony of how my dad's extraordinary vision for his family, grew wings and flourished. Unfortunately that's not what occurred. I have no doubt that my father had a plan for what he was trying to build, but somehow the details for continuing his efforts were not communicated to the point of sustainability. My dad spent the better part of thirty years strategizing to put his family in a better financial position. From the day I was born, I never knew my dad to have less than three jobs. He was a Plant Operator for the Kansas City Kansas Public Schools USD 500, the owner/contractor for McConnell Cleaning & Janitorial Service, and the proprietor of Johnnie McConnell Properties LLC. The first two jobs empowered him to be able to do what I believe he enjoyed the most - buying property. With each house my dad acquired, it seemed fulfillment grew within him. He was so focused on the journey, that he didn't take the time to make sure our family had a handle on his vision. Including the home we lived in, my father had amassed fourteen houses. He never bought a house with the intention of selling it. The whole family was part of the restoration crew. Uncle Calvin, one of my father's brothers, was contracted to do any work that was beyond us (which was a lot). All of my dad's houses were rental properties. When he wasn't working the other two jobs, he was collecting rent or responding to renters' maintenance issues. I had a front row seat, witnessing my dad as part of our community's solution. He employed extended family members to work the eight cleaning contracts, and he rented houses to people who might not have qualified on a standard application. My dad's financial portfolio was so strong that when the King Solomon Baptist Church building became the property of the bank, he bought the building, securing a mortgage for my Uncle Mack as the first home of Third Street Baptist Church.

He had heart failure, and his death caught us by surprise. We rallied as a family should, but some matters were more complicated than any of us realized at the time. As we went back to living our own lives, we couldn't appreciate the weight of everything that had fallen on our mother. It all began to spin out of control, and within eighteen months she filed bankruptcy. The houses that should have been our legacy, were now gone.

The lesson I learned was, a vision cannot last without proper support. It must be adequately communicated so that those who embrace it can run with it. Like my dad, I've experienced my purpose/vision as fuel for living. At times I'm so immersed in the writing process, that I lose sight of the importance of implementing a wealth building component. It's part of what contributed to my divorce. Sometimes visionaries get stuck on the creation side of things. We're being fulfilled while everyone connected to us is waiting for the sustainability part to kick in. I couldn't truly appreciate that perspective until now. What good is having a portfolio of three thousand songs, if there is no transactional mechanism in place for growth or sustainability?

Moving from the conceptualization to the actualization of a vision requires a multifaceted approach that integrates strategic planning, effective leadership, resource management, adaptability, and stakeholder engagement.

Here's a comprehensive exploration of what is required for a vision to go from conceptualization to actualization.

1. Clear Vision and Goals

A vision must start with a clear and compelling idea of what the end goal looks like. This involves defining the purpose, mission, and values that underpin the vision. Goals should be specific, measurable, achievable, relevant, and time-bound. Clarity ensures that everyone involved understands the destination and the steps needed to get there.

2. Leadership and Commitment

Strong leadership is essential to drive the vision forward. Leaders inspire and motivate others, communicate the vision effectively, and make strategic decisions to overcome challenges. Commitment from leaders fosters dedication throughout the organization and encourages perseverance during setbacks.

3. Strategic Planning

Strategic planning translates the vision into actionable steps. This involves analyzing the current situation, identifying opportunities and threats, setting priorities, allocating resources, and developing timelines. A well-defined strategy provides a roadmap that guides decision-making and resource allocation.

4. Effective Communication

Clear and consistent communication is crucial at every stage of the journey. Leaders must articulate the vision, goals, and expectations to stakeholders within and outside the organization. Effective communication fosters understanding, alignment, and engagement, motivating individuals to contribute towards the vision's realization.

5. Resource Allocation and Management

Resources—including financial, human, and technological—are essential for executing the vision. Effective resource management involves budgeting, allocating resources based on priorities, optimizing efficiency, and adapting resource allocation as needed throughout the process. Adequate resources ensure that initiatives can progress without unnecessary delays.

6. Team Building and Empowerment

Building a capable and motivated team is key to executing the vision. This involves recruiting individuals with the right skills and mindset, fostering collaboration and trust among team members, and empowering them to take ownership of their responsibilities. A cohesive team can innovate, problem-solve, and adapt to challenges more effectively.

7. Adaptability and Flexibility

The journey towards actualizing a vision is rarely linear. Organizations must remain adaptable and flexible in response to changing circumstances, market dynamics, and unforeseen challenges. This requires openness to new ideas, willingness to revise strategies, and agility in implementing adjustments without losing sight of the overarching vision.

8. Continuous Evaluation and Improvement

Regular evaluation of progress against goals is essential for course correction and improvement. This involves collecting and analyzing data, soliciting feedback from stakeholders, identifying areas for improvement, and celebrating milestones. Continuous evaluation ensures that the vision remains relevant and achievable throughout its implementation.

9. Risk Management

Identifying and mitigating risks is crucial to minimize potential disruptions and setbacks. Risk management involves assessing potential risks, developing contingency plans, and implementing measures to reduce their impact. Proactive risk management safeguards the progress towards achieving the vision.

10. Cultural Alignment

Aligning organizational culture with the vision enhances cohesion and commitment. This involves fostering a culture that values innovation, collaboration, integrity, and accountability. When the organizational culture aligns with the vision, individuals are more likely to embrace change, work towards common goals, and contribute positively to the vision's realization.

11. Stakeholder Engagement

Engaging stakeholders—including employees, customers, investors, and community members—is crucial for garnering support and feedback. Effective stakeholder engagement involves listening to stakeholders' perspectives, addressing their concerns, and involving them in decision-making where appropriate. Engaged stakeholders become advocates for the vision and contribute to its success.

12. Celebration and Recognition

Celebrating achievements, milestones, and successes along the journey boosts morale and reinforces commitment to the vision. Recognition of individuals and teams who contribute to the vision's realization fosters a positive work environment and motivates continued effort towards the final goal.

CHAPTER X

THE END IS NOT YOUR BUSINESS

A Pattern to Live By

The Johnnie McConnell Family

Standing Left to Right: Mark, Shirley, Janice and John
Front Row: Dennis, Johnnie, Jimmie and Christopher

Johnnie is the fifth son born to the late Mack and Macie McConnell. Born in Vernon, Louisiana, he moved to Kansas City, Kansas in 1951 and participated in the "lucrative" business of the Kansas City Flood Cleanup project. He returned to Louisiana a few months later to take a bride, the former Jimmie Mae Grimes of Lillie, La. They were married on August 16, 1952 and returned to Kansas City the next day—August 17. Johnnie was employed a short period of time at the Fulton Bag Company and for the next twelve years at the Nutrena Feed Mill. Afterwards, he became employed in the Kansas City, Kansas Public School System.

Today, Johnnie is still with the school system as well as operating his own business of two years—McConnell's Cleaning and Janitorial Service.

Johnnie and Jimmie are the parents of six children—Shirley Ann, age 14; Mark Allen, age 13; Janice Marie, age 10; John David, age 8; Dennis James, age 6; and Christopher Lloyd, age 5. Another son, Carlton Dwight, passed away at the age of 11 in 1971.

The entire family are active members of the Mt. Zion Baptist Church in Kansas City, Kansas where Rev. C.L. Bachus is Pastor. Johnnie is Chairman of the Deacon Board, Jimmie Mae sings in the Senior Choir (you ought to hear her leading such favorites as "Jesus Can Work it Out," "I Know Prayer Changes Things," and "Lift Him Up.") The children serve on the Jr. Usher Board as well as sing in the children's and junior choir.

Worrying about how things will end is an anti-ingredient for living well. As deputies of God, we've been assigned to create (opportunities, relationships, etc.). To fear something's end while in the throes of creating it, is counterproductive. It's an oxymoron.

A key reason for making sure your vision is well communicated, is so that worry is taken completely off the table. Although fear is a great motivator for change, it shouldn't be relied on as a permanent strategy. Fear of a stroke and heart attack made me exercise more to lose weight, but my desire to live healthier caused me to change my lifestyle. The best of how we live must somehow become intrinsically motivated. We dramatically affect the end by how we choose to participate in the moment. We write the lines, but not the story. There's no way to control how each moment will judge us, so take that off your list. Live out loud, and on purpose be who you are! The truth is, you'll never know your legacy. By definition, it's what you leave to others. A Yiddish proverb says, "man plans, God laughs".

For many of us, we don't have enough years left to live down some of the things we've done. Live to please God. - not to satisfy those who stand in judgment.

Focusing on beginnings rather than endings offers a profound perspective on life and productivity. Whether applied to personal growth, projects, relationships, or any endeavor, this approach cultivates optimism, innovation, and resilience. By understanding the significance of beginnings, individuals can harness their energy more effectively and navigate challenges with greater clarity and determination.

Beginnings signify a fresh start and a blank canvas. They represent a moment of limitless potential and opportunity. When embarking on a new journey, whether it's starting a new job, initiating a project, or even making a lifestyle change, the beginning is where intentions are set and visions are crafted. This initial phase allows individuals to define their goals clearly and establish the necessary groundwork for success. For instance, when starting a new job, focusing on the beginning enables one to learn and adapt quickly, building a strong foundation for future growth and achievement.

Beginnings also foster creativity and innovation. In the early stages of any venture, there is an openness to explore new ideas and approaches. This creative energy is essential for problem-solving and generating innovative solutions. By immersing oneself in the process of creation and exploration, individuals can discover unexpected opportunities and avenues for development. In the realm of entrepreneurship, entrepreneurs often find that focusing on the beginning allows them to experiment with different business models and strategies, leading to breakthrough innovations.

Resilience and adaptability are cultivated during the initial stages of a project or endeavor. The infancy period provides opportunities to learn from mistakes and setbacks, fostering personal growth and development. When faced with challenges or obstacles, individuals who focus on beginnings are better equipped to persevere and find alternative paths to success. By maintaining a positive mindset and embracing the learning process inherent in beginnings, we can build tenacity and perseverance, essential qualities for long-term success. When people focus on getting things started, they are more likely to be fully engaged in the present, rather than dwelling on past failures or anxiously anticipating future outcomes. This focus enhances productivity and fosters a sense of fulfillment and satisfaction in one's actions. Athletes and performers often emphasize the importance of focusing on the beginning of every practice or performance, as it allows them to function at their best and achieve optimal results.

Connections and relationships are better facilitated at the start of something new. Whether it's starting a new friendship, embarking on a romantic relationship, or initiating a collaboration, focusing on the beginning creates a foundation for trust, communication, and mutual understanding. By investing time and energy in building positive connections from the outset, individuals can cultivate strong and supportive relationships that endure over time.

Worrying about the end, whether it's the conclusion of a project, a performance, or even life itself, can induce performance anxiety by creating excessive pressure to achieve perfection or avoid failure. The fear of falling short of expectations or not meeting one's own standards amplifies stress and diminishes focus. This anxiety often stems from a fixation on potential negative outcomes, leading to self-doubt and second-guessing. It disrupts the natural flow of creativity and capability, overshadowing preparation and skill. Managing such anxiety involves shifting focus to the present moment, embracing challenges as opportunities for growth, and fostering a supportive mindset.

When I began writing this book, I knew from the onset that it wouldn't be a traditional biography. Although meaningful, I chose not to attempt to chronologize all of the important events that occurred in my dad's life. When a person has lived well, it's impossible to capture every meaningful moment. A true biography of the life of Johnnie McConnell would require no less than 1000 pages. There's no attempt on my part to portray the memory of my dad from any lens other than my own. I don't believe his story can be told in one book, by one person. It's imperative to me that every reader understands that this book does not represent my dad's story. This manuscript represents connections for life lessons I've learned by simply walking in my dad's shadow (likeness/image). My father's impact was so individual and consequential, that if my siblings wrote their own books about our father, they would introduce layers of him that I've not mentioned.

A segment of our population identifies with the philosophy of doomsday preppers - which is a complex and multifaceted phenomenon, driven by a combination of historical, cultural, psychological, and philosophical factors. At its core, prepping reflects deep-seated fears and uncertainties about the future, combined with a desire for control, self-reliance, and existential meaning. While prepping can provide individuals with a sense of security and empowerment, it also raises important questions about societal trust, resource allocation, and the nature of preparedness itself. Ultimately, the focus on the end within doomsday prepping can be understood as both a response to real and perceived threats and a reflection of broader existential concerns. As we navigate an increasingly uncertain world, the philosophy of prepping challenges us to consider not only how we prepare for the worst but also how we address the underlying causes of our fears and work towards a more resilient and equitable future.

When life deals you a heavy blow and knocks you on the canvas, you must choose whether or not to get back up. In professional boxing, when a boxer is caught off guard and knocked down, he sometimes gets up too quickly. The legs can't quite figure out their role, and the eyes are totally glossed over. In this condition, it's almost inevitable that the fighter will be going down just as quickly again. Surviving any knockdown in a boxing ring, or in the ring of life, is contingent upon not only IF you get back up, but HOW you go about it. Unless you're ready for ensuing challenges, defeat will be your next chapter.

Counting the cost is a fundamental aspect of strategic decision-making. By carefully evaluating the financial, emotional, time, and resource implications, individuals can make informed choices that align with their goals and capacities. This thoughtful approach not only minimizes potential risks but also maximizes the chances of achieving successful outcomes. Whether in business, career, or personal life, understanding and preparing for the costs associated with challenging endeavors, is essential for achieving long-term success and fulfillment.

Successfully managing to recover from a knockdown in a boxing match requires a combination of mental resilience, strategic thinking, and physical recovery techniques. The fighter must quickly regain composure and refocus. Maintaining a calm and collected mindset is essential in combating panic and disorientation. Imagine yourself getting back on your feet and taking control of the fight. After hitting the canvas, the fighter should stay composed and assess their physical condition. If necessary, use the

10-count from the referee to gather strength and assess how the opponent is reacting. It's vital to avoid getting up too quickly, which can lead to a more severe injury.

The referee's count is crucial here—aim to rise by the count of eight to ensure you're ready to continue. Once back on your feet, the primary focus should be on defense. Avoid aggressive exchanges immediately after getting up, as this can leave you vulnerable to another knockdown. Good footwork and head movement are critical to avoid further hits and regain your rhythm. Gradually work to reassert control over the fight. Focus on your strengths and use effective strategies to counter the opponent's aggression.

Between rounds, the corner team plays a vital role. Listening to their guidance and following their tactical adjustments can greatly aid in turning the fight around.

Lastly, recovering from a knockdown effectively is greatly enhanced by rigorous training. Sparring with situations that mimic being knocked down or under pressure can build resilience and improve a fighter's ability to handle real fight scenarios.

It wasn't a fluke that my parents had as many kids as they did. They took into account all that it would entail, and still proceeded. Unfortunately, doing your due diligence and weighing risk factors, doesn't guarantee the results we're necessarily seeking. My dad modeled for me how to live life expecting, but not expecting a guarantee. Nothing is guaranteed, but the energy you expend going towards your focus moves the needle.

The power of expecting is a dynamic force that influences our lives in profound ways. From personal growth and professional success to social interactions and organizational culture, expectations shape our experiences and outcomes. By understanding and harnessing the power of expectation, individuals and organizations can drive positive change, achieve remarkable results, and create environments where high expectations lead to growth and success. Embracing the potential of expectation allows us to unlock our full capabilities and transform our lives and the lives of those around us.

My parents' expectation was to bring six lives into the world. I'm sure they never imagined having to lose their first six children. That's like the worst case scenario with 0.999% probability. My father never trained for a professional boxing bout, nor did he stock a bunker in preparation for the end of the world. Those were not his experiences, but somehow he managed to teach me both the risks and rewards of finding a balance in life. Lessons are only wasted when you don't learn from them, so my take away is, to never abandon your hope.

Dr. John D. McConnell

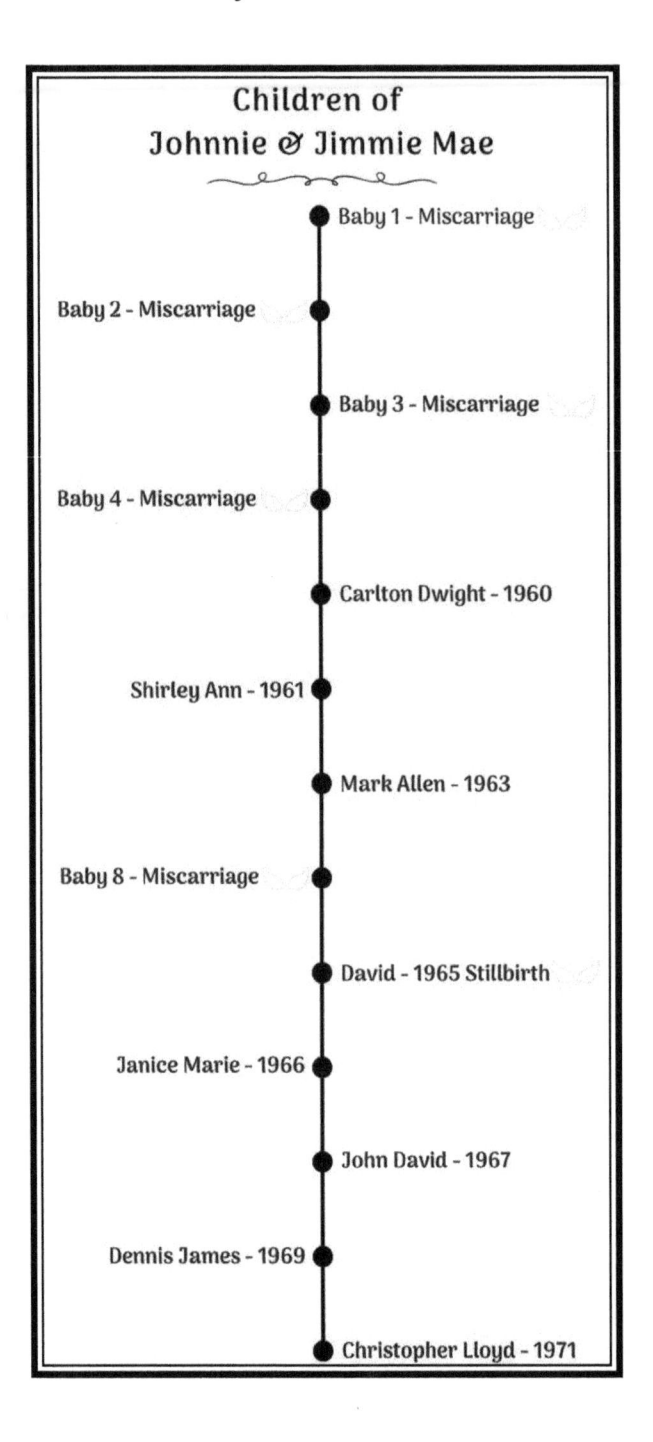

Children of Johnnie & Jimmie Mae

- Baby 1 - Miscarriage
- Baby 2 - Miscarriage
- Baby 3 - Miscarriage
- Baby 4 - Miscarriage
- Carlton Dwight - 1960
- Shirley Ann - 1961
- Mark Allen - 1963
- Baby 8 - Miscarriage
- David - 1965 Stillbirth
- Janice Marie - 1966
- John David - 1967
- Dennis James - 1969
- Christopher Lloyd - 1971

A Pattern to Live By

IN HIS IMAGE

A Pattern to Live By

ABOUT THE AUTHOR

Dr. John David McConnell is the owner of Prolyric Productions Publishing Company. Born and raised in Kansas City Kansas, John received his Bachelor of Science degree at Saint Mary College in Leavenworth, Kansas. John taught grades 2 through 8 over the span of his 27-year career as a public-school educator. 20 of those years were with the Houston Independent School District.

In 2016 John received his doctorate in sacred music from Christian Bible Institute & Seminary. His war chest of badges includes Christian, father of two sons, educator, actor, singer, songwriter, worship-leader, Certified Christian Counselor, and author. John exited his teaching career in 2022, and is currently pursuing his literary and songwriting careers full-time.

Other Books by John McConnell:
Motivated/ A Journal Of The Journey
From The Front Lines
Losing Sight But Not Vision
Imagine You Have It
Winning At Being You
Time/The Great Equalizer

Contact info:
johndmac4@aol.com
832-865-0260

Left to right – youngest to oldest: James Daniel, Clemontain, Jura Dean, Lerlene, Pearlene, Mack Jr. Theo, Cleo, Johnnie, Lonnie, Calvester, Houston, Lloyd, Nita Mae

A Pattern to Live By

Milton Keynes UK
Ingram Content Group UK Ltd.
UKHW051413011224
451809UK00018B/146

9 798823 036269